Learn to Sign the Fun Way!

PENNY WARNER

Learn to Sign the Fun Way!

LET YOUR FINGERS DO THE TALKING WITH GAMES, PUZZLES, AND ACTIVITIES IN AMERICAN SIGN LANGUAGE

THREE RIVERS PRESS
NEW YORK

To Tom, Matt, and Rebecca

Published by Three Rivers Press, New York, New York.
Member of the Crown Publishing Group, a division of Random House, Inc.
www.randomhouse.com

THREE RIVERS PRESS and the Tugboat design are registered trademarks of Random House, Inc.

Originally published by Prima Publishing, Roseville, California, in 2001.

Interior illustrations by Paula Gray and Laurie Baker-McNeile

Printed in the United States of America

Library of Congress Cataloging-in-Publication Data
Warner, Penny.
Learn to sign the fun way : let your fingers do the talking with games, puzzles, and activities in American Sign Language / Penny Warner.
      p.   cm.
   Includes index.
     1. American Sign Language. 2. Educational games. I. Title.
HV2474.W37   2001
419.7—dc21   2001021084

ISBN 0-7615-3263-3

20 19 18 17 16 15 14 13 12

First Edition

Contents

Acknowledgments

Thanks to the following teachers who inspired my love for sign language: Linda Barde, Neil Christiansen, Peggy Garvin, and Beverly Wilson.

Thanks also to Diana Todd for a fun idea. And a special thanks to my wonderful editor, Jamie Miller.

Introduction

Welcome to *Learn to Sign the Fun Way!* You're about to learn an exciting new language that will teach you how to "talk" with your hands. Soon you'll be able to "say" the alphabet with your fingers; use your hands to shape words; and express whole sentences, thoughts, and feelings through American Sign Language (ASL).

ASL, used primarily by deaf people, is the fourth most common language in the United States. It's accepted by most colleges as a foreign language and is offered at many high schools today. You can learn this visually beautiful language by studying the signs, practicing the sentences, and playing the games in *Learn to Sign the Fun Way!*

Sign language is easy to learn. Just look at the illustrations provided in the book and read the descriptions to make sure you're doing the signs correctly. Soon you'll be signing hundreds of words and having conversations. Sign language comes in "handy" in many ways, especially when you don't want to talk out loud. It's even better if you learn to sign with your friends. That way you will have someone to sign to and can practice your skills together. And if you should meet a deaf person, you'll be able to communicate. In fact, if you get really good at sign language, you might even want to make a career of it, by becoming an interpreter for the deaf.

Most of all, learning sign language is fun. I learned the manual alphabet in sixth grade and never forgot it. Eventually I took sign language classes, became fluent, and got my master's degree in special education for the deaf. I've taught sign language to students for more than twenty years, just because it's fun to teach and fun for students to learn. Sign language is like using a code to talk with others who also know the code, so you can chat in private any time you like. The hand shapes often look like familiar gestures, so they're easy to remember. And with practice, you'll soon be singing songs, telling jokes, and playing games in sign language.

Learn to Sign the Fun Way! consists of eighteen chapters filled with illustrated signs to learn, and a last chapter packed with sign language games. Chapter 1 offers basic information about American Sign Language and tips on how to use the signs. Chapter 2 teaches you fingerspelling, also known as the manual alphabet, with practice exercises at the end to help you learn the letters *A* through *Z.* In chapter 3 you'll find the numbers 0 through 10, then 20 through 100 counting by tens, and a few extra numbers you may also need. This chapter also includes practice exercises to help you learn your numbers.

You'll begin to learn signs in chapter 4, starting with people signs, such as your relatives and friends. Chapter 5 is loaded with easy-to-learn animal signs, everything from backyard pets to wild animals at the zoo. You'll find signs for food and drink in chapter 6—all your favorites from *pizza* and *hamburgers* to *candy* and *gum.*

In chapter 7 you'll learn home signs, for things you see around the house. Chapter 8 gives you clothing signs so you can talk about what you're wearing, and chapter 9 teaches color signs so you can tell your friends your favorite colors. Chapter 10 is full of sport signs, such as *baseball* and *soccer,* while chapter 11 offers activity signs, such as *dance* and *play.*

Chapter 12 will teach you how to express your thoughts, and chapter 13 offers signs to help you express your feelings. Chapter 14 provides action signs, such as *come* and *go, walk* and *talk, work* and *sleep.* Chapter

15 includes body signs, so you can talk about your head, hands, or heart.

In chapter 16 you'll find school signs, so you can discuss your teacher, homework, or computer. Chapter 17 gives you calendar signs, including time of day and days of the week, and chapter 18 offers lots of silly and fun signs, everything from *cute* and *funny* to *stinky* and *ugly*.

Each chapter offers practice exercises to help you increase your skills and speed. Lots of added tips and information are included throughout the book, to help you learn more about American Sign Language, deaf people, and deaf culture.

When you've finished learning the signs, it's time to play some games using sign language. Chapter 19 describes more than 80 great games to play with your friends or by yourself. Get ready to try your "hand" at "Daffy Deaf-initions," "Funny Fingerspelling," and "Guess the Gesture," among others.

If you want to continue learning signs when you're finished with the book, check out the Resources at the back. There's also a glossary to help you understand some of the terms used in the chapters and an index to help you find the word you're looking for.

All you need to get started besides the book are your fingers and hands. So turn the page—it's time to *Learn to Sign the Fun Way!*

CHAPTER 1

American Sign Language

Eight-year-old Connor Westphal can't hear her mother laugh, her dog bark, or her friends say "Hello," but she understands a joke when her mother explains it in sign language. She senses her dog's excitement by his snapping head and wagging tail. And she recognizes her friends' greetings by their big smiles and waves.

Connor is deaf. She was born hearing but contracted meningitis when she was only a year old. Although she heard sounds and speech before she

How Many Deaf People Are There?

Twenty million people in the United States have a hearing loss. Two million are considered deaf, and many of them use sign language. If a person is deaf, he or she cannot hear or understand speech or most sounds in the environment, even with a hearing aid. Deafness can be caused by heredity, illness, abnormalities, head injury, some medications, and aging. Some forms of deafness can be corrected by surgery, hearing aids, or cochlear implants.

Some hearing people confuse "Braille" and "sign language." Braille is not a language; it's a tactile system of raised dots on paper that represent letters and enable blind people to read. Sign language is a visual language used by many deaf people to communicate.

became deaf, she can't remember hearing anything. She had even begun to say a few words—*Dada, Doggy,* and *Juice.* But she stopped talking after her illness.

When Connor's parents realized she was deaf, they enrolled her in an infant program for children with hearing impairments. She began to learn American Sign Language, known as ASL. And she began to "talk" again, using her hands to shape words and phrases. "Dada" became an open hand tapped at the forehead. "Doggy" was a snapped finger and a pat on the leg. And "juice" was an open fist squeezed shut at her mouth.

Sign language changed Connor's life. It took her from the world of silence to the world of communication, just like it has for thousands of deaf people in the United States.

American Sign Language is a visual language, different from American Indian Sign Language, scuba diver sign language, army sign language, even British Sign Language. It is one of the most expressive languages, using not only the hands but gestures, body language, facial expressions, and manual signs as well. ASL is the fourth most common language in the United States and is now accepted in many states as a college language requirement. Many high schools today offer sign language for credit.

What Is an Interpreter?

A sign language interpreter translates speech into sign language for a deaf person and sign language into speech for a hearing person. Hearing people who know sign language have many job opportunities, such as teaching, counseling, and interpreting. The most common places to interpret are in court, at hospitals, in classrooms, and at public gatherings.

Most of all, sign language is fun to learn and fun to use. You can talk to your friends without anyone "overhearing" you. You can chat across a football field when it's too noisy to shout. You can sign underwater, in the library, at the movies, or any time you want to keep the conversation private or quiet.

First you need to learn the manual alphabet, also known as *fingerspelling,* shown in chapter 2. Practice the letters a while so you know them by heart. Then learn the fun signs featured in the book to get you started in American Sign Language. When you've learned the alphabet and signs, play the games and activities in the last chapter with friends who have also learned sign language.

CHAPTER 2
The Manual Alphabet

Fingerspelling is also called the *manual alphabet,* because it uses the fingers to make letters, one at a time. Each letter is represented by a specific hand shape. Once you know the alphabet, you can communicate with anyone else who knows the manual alphabet, by spelling out words. And you can spell out words if you don't know the signs.

Here are some tips for better fingerspelling:

1. Use fingerspelling when you don't know the sign.
2. Hold your hand palm out, facing the reader.
3. Keep your hand relaxed and steady. Make your letters clear and smooth so they're easy to read. Don't bounce or jerk your hand.
4. Don't block your face or mouth; this way the reader can see your lips and facial expression.
5. Pause for a second at the end of a word, but don't drop your hand.
6. For double letters, make a small bounce, sign the letter twice, or glide the letter to the side a little.
7. Try to read fingerspelling in syllables, not as letters. Try to spell the word as a whole, not one letter at a time.
8. Practice fingerspelling road signs, book titles, and simple phrases throughout the day.

Which Hand Should I Use?

Use your dominant hand to make most of the signs. If you're right-handed, use your right hand. If you're left-handed, use your left hand. If you're ambidextrous and use both hands equally, choose one hand to use for finger-spelling and stay with it. Don't change hands back and forth.

Fingerspelling: The Manual Alphabet

A

Make a flat fist.

B

Place thumb in palm, fingers straight up.

C

Make C shape.

D

Place index finger straight up; make O with fingers and thumb.

E

Place fingertips flat against thumb.

F

Make *O* with thumb and
index finger; close fingers.

G

Make fist; stick index finger
and thumb out.

H

Place index and middle
fingers together, sideways.

I

Stick baby finger up.

J

Make baby finger shape *J*.

K

Place index and middle finger
straight; rest thumb
between the two fingers.

L

Make *L* shape with index finger and thumb.

Did You Know?

Deaf people in the United States use a one-handed manual alphabet, while British deaf people use a two-handed alphabet.

M

Stick thumb out from under three fingers.

N

Stick thumb out from under two fingers.

O

Shape *O* with fingers
and thumb.

P

Make *K*; turn down.

Q

Make *G*; turn down.

R

Cross index and middle fingers.

S

Make fist, place thumb on top of fingers.

T

Stick thumb out between index and middle fingers.

U

Stick index and middle finger straight up.

V

Make *V* with index and middle fingers.

W

Make *W* with three fingers.

X

Crook index finger;
curl others.

Y

Make *Y* by sticking out
thumb and baby finger.

Z

Draw *Z* with index finger.

Try the following:

1. Spell the alphabet as fast as you can. Time yourself. Repeat ten times and see whether you get faster by the tenth time.
2. Spell your whole name.
3. Spell your name backward.
4. Spell the names of your family members.
5. Spell the names of your friends.
6. Spell the words on the back of a cereal box or in a magazine.
7. Spell a line from a favorite song from memory or as you listen to the radio.
8. Spell signs you see as you ride in the car.
9. Spell your school spelling list for double practice.
10. Spell out a whole sentence.
11. Have a conversation fingerspelling with a friend who also knows the manual alphabet.

Which Way Is Up?

Be sure to hold your hands facing the person who's reading you so he or she can see your signs clearly. After all, you already know what you're saying! Don't make your signs too large or exaggerated or the reader won't be able to follow along. Keep your hands close to your chest, and make your arm movements small so you aren't "shouting" at your reader.

CHAPTER 3

Number Signs

American Sign Language number signs are similar to hand gestures used by hearing people, but there are some important differences. The numbers 1, 2, 4, and 5 are the same, but 3 is different. And instead of using two hands for the numbers 6 through 10, you use one hand to sign them. Once you learn the numbers from 1 to 10, then 20 through 100, you'll be able to sign any number from 1 to infinity!

The Seven Basic Hand Shapes

Seven basic hand shapes are used to make most signs.

and or flat *O* hand

Hand shaped like a flattened letter *O*.

flat hand

Hand open and flat, with
fingers together.

open hand

Hand shaped like the
number 5, fingers spread.

bent hand

Hand bent at a 45- to
90-degree angle.

curved hand

Hand shaped like the letter C.

closed hand

Hand shaped like a fist.

clawed hand

Hand shaped like a claw,
with fingers bent and spread.

Numbers

Sign the numbers 1 through 5 facing inward.

1

Hold up index finger.

2

Hold up *V.*

3

Hold up thumb and *V.*

4

Hold up four fingers.

5

Hold up and spread four fingers and thumb.

Make the signs from 6 to 9 facing outward.

6

Touch thumb to tip of baby finger.

7

Touch thumb to tip
of ring finger.

8

Touch thumb to tip of
middle finger.

9

Touch thumb to tip
of index finger.

10

Make *A* with thumb pointing up; wiggle slightly.

Make the signs from 11 to 15 facing inward.

11

Flick *1* twice.

12

Flick *2* twice.

13

Bend *3* inward twice.

14

Bend *4* inward twice.

15

Bend *5* inward twice.

Make the signs from 16 to 19 by starting with the A sign facing you, then turning your head outward to make the number.

16

Twist *A* out to 6.

17

Twist *A* out to 7.

18

Twist *A* out to 8.

Did You Know?

It's not easy to read lips. It takes training and practice, and even then many deaf people can only recognize between 35 and 70 percent of the speech. Lipreading is even more difficult when the person speaking has a mustache, is chewing gum, slurs words, mumbles, or moves the lips in an exaggerated way.

19

Twist *A* out to *9*.

Make the signs from 30 to 90, counting by tens, by making the number and adding 0. The exception is 20.

20

Touch thumb to index fingertip twice.

30

Make *3* then *0*.

40

Make *4* then *0*.

50

Make *5* then *0*.

60

Make *6* then *0*.

70

Make *7* then *0*.

80

Make *8* then *0*.

90

Make *9* then *0*.

100

Make *1* then *C*.

1,000

Make *1* and then tap fingertips into other palm.

0

Make 0.

number

Make two flat *0*s; twist at fingertips.

How to Sign Numbers

When signing round numbers like 30 or 50, sign the number + zero. But when signing numbers like 34 or 55, sign each number, such as 3 then 4 or 5 then 5. Do *not* sign the 0 implied by 30 or 50 in our example.

Sign the following as if you'd say them in English:

- Money amounts, such as $1.75, would be signed "one dollar and seventy-five cents" (sign 75, not 7-0-5).
- Years, such as 1981, would be signed 19 + 8 + 1. 2001 would be signed 2 + 1,000 + 1.
- Numbers in addresses, such as 710 Sinnet Court, would be signed 7 + 10.
- Telephone numbers, such as 837-7089, would be signed 8 + 3 + 7 + 7 + 0 + 8 + 9 individually.

Sign your age by first placing an *A* on your chin, then as you move your hand down, sign the numbers in your age.

Try the following number activities:
1. Count to 10.
2. Count backward from 10 to 1.
3. Count to 20.
4. Count to 100 by 10s.
5. Count all the way to 100.
6. Sign your age.

7. Sign the ages of your family members.

8. Sign your address.

9. Sign your phone number.

10. Sign your best friend's phone number.

11. Sign your birth date and year.

12. Sign how much money you have.

13. Sign the problems and answers to your math homework.

14. Sign the numbers you see while riding in the car.

15. Sign the numbers that appear on TV.

16. Practice your math problems with a friend who knows sign language.

CHAPTER 4
People Signs

People signs are often placed on different parts of the face, according to whether they are male or female, such as "man," "woman," "girl," and "boy." The male signs are placed on or near the upper half the face, while the female signs are placed on or near the lower half of the face. The signs are based on the hats that children wore in the past—the boy's cap with visor represents the sign for "boy," and the string of the girl's bonnet along the cheek represents the sign for "girl."

Did You Know?

Parents are beginning to teach their babies sign language, to help them learn to speak. Giving abstract words a physical form seems to give babies assistance in learning concepts and vocalizing.

people

Circle *P* fingers,
alternately.

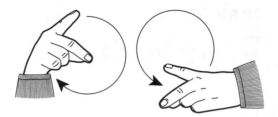

friend

Hook index fingers; reverse.

you

Point to the person
you're talking to.

me

Point to yourself.

dad

Touch forehead with thumb of 5.

mom

Touch chin with thumb of 5.

grandfather

Make *father,* then
move outward.

grandmother

Make *mother,* then move
outward.

son

Touch forehead; then
sign *baby* (page 37).

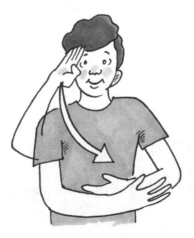

daughter

Touch chin; then sign *baby* (page 37).

brother

Point to forehead; then put *L* on *L*.

sister

Point to chin; then put *L* on *L*.

man

Touch *5* to forehead,
then chest.

woman

Touch *5* to chin, then chest.

boy

Make flat *O* on forehead.

girl

Brush cheek with A.

baby

Cradle baby with arms.

kid

Rub under nose with 1.

parents

Tap *5* to forehead, then chin.

family

Make two *F*s, fingertips touching; make circle outward.

Try the following sentences using fingerspelling and signs:

1. My friends are good people.
2. Would you give that to me?
3. Dad and Mom like to take long trips.
4. My grandfather lives with my grandmother.
5. Her son is Matt, and her daughter is Sue.
6. I have a brother, but I don't have a sister.
7. The tall man is next to the short woman.
8. A boy and a girl are playing outside.
9. I have a baby brother and a kid sister.
10. My parents are part of my family.

Do You Have a Question?

If you're signing a question, you should use a questioning face, by raising your eyebrows and leaning your head forward slightly. Or you can draw a question mark at the end of the sentence with your index finger.

CHAPTER 5
Animal Signs

Animal signs are easy to remember because they often feature a characteristic of the specific animal. For example, the "monkey" sign is made by scratching your sides, the "horse" sign is made by flopping over "ears," and the "cat" sign is a pull of the "whiskers." For fun, learn the animal signs, then have your nonsigning friends guess the animal when you make the sign.

The Deaf Community

People who use the same language and share common interests form the Deaf community. Many work for the rights of deaf people, such as having equal opportunities for jobs, accepting American Sign Language as a recognized language, and including TTYs—teletypewriter devices for the deaf—in public places so deaf people can use the phone.

animal

Put fingertips on chest;
bend hands.

horse

Place *U* on head, facing
outward; bend down.

cat

Pull "whiskers" with
F from mouth.

dog

Snap fingers; tap leg.

tiger

Pull bent claw hands out at face, like stripes.

lion

Wiggle claw C back over head, like a mane.

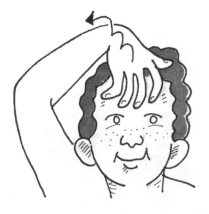

bear

Cross arms in front of
yourself; scratch.

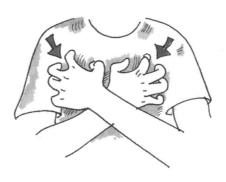

snake

Make bent *V*; zigzag out
from mouth.

monkey

Scratch sides like a monkey.

elephant

Dip *U* down from nose,
like a trunk.

bug

Place thumb of *3* on nose;
wiggle fingers.

turtle

Cover *A* hand with other
hand; wiggle thumb.

COW

Twist *Y* forward on top of head.

pig

Flap *B* under chin.

mouse

Brush *1* on tip of nose.

bird

Open *V* and close at mouth,
like a beak.

frog

Flick *V* out from under
chin, like a throat.

fish

Wiggle *B* forward,
like a fish.

Try the following sentences using fingerspelling and signs:

1. My favorite animal is a horse.
2. Do you have a cat or a dog?
3. I like tigers but not lions.
4. You have a teddy bear, and I have a stuffed snake.
5. There are more monkeys in the jungle than elephants.
6. I saw a rabbit that looked like a skunk.
7. Cows and pigs like to stand in the mud.
8. Which is smaller, a mouse or a bird?
9. Can a frog breathe underwater like a fish?

Did You Know?

Sometimes when a hearing person telephones a deaf person, he may hear an electronic sound. That means the phone is a TTY, a teletypewriter device, and the caller needs a TTY to communicate with him.

CHAPTER 6
Food and Drink Signs

Many of the food signs will remind you of the actual foods they represent, such as "making a hamburger patty" and "peeling a banana." That makes them easier to memorize. Picture the food as you sign the word to help you remember it.

Did You Know?

Some hearing people don't know how to interact with deaf people. They ignore them, shout at them, or treat them as if they are not very bright. You should communicate directly with a deaf person, talk normally, and realize deaf people are just as smart as hearing people.

breakfast

Circle *B* around side
of mouth.

lunch

Circle *L* around side of
mouth.

dinner

Circle *D* around side
of mouth.

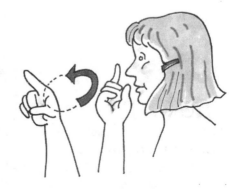

snack

Put hand to mouth; snap outward.

bread

Hand slices back of other hand.

butter

Brush palm with *U*.

meat

Pinch *F* between thumb
and index finger.

pizza

Bend *V* and shape *Z* in air.

sandwich

Press hands together;
lift toward mouth.

french fries

Bounce two *F*s.

hamburger

Clasp hands; reverse.

hot dog

Squeeze fingers open and close, moving apart like sausage links.

apple

Twist an *A* in your cheek.

banana

Imitate peeling your
index finger.

ice cream

Lick an ice cream cone.

cookies

Cut out cookies on palm with *C* claw.

candy

Twist *1* into cheek.

gum

Bend *N* into cheek.

water

Tap *W* at chin.

milk

Squeeze fists like milking
a cow.

juice

Squeeze fists at mouth.

soda

Touch arm with *1*.

tea

Stir *F* on top of *O*.

coffee

Grind two fists, one on top of the other.

food /eat

Tap mouth with flat O.

drink

Imitate pouring drink in mouth.

Try the following sentences using fingerspelling and signs:
1. I like breakfast more than lunch.
2. I sometimes have a snack before dinner.
3. Do you like butter on your bread?
4. My dad eats meat, but I like pizza.
5. I prefer french fries with my sandwich.
6. Do you want a hamburger or a hot dog?

7. Apples and bananas are good for your health.
8. I like a cookie with my ice cream.
9. My dentist doesn't eat candy or chew gum.
10. I drink water at school and milk with meals.
11. Juice is better for you than soda.
12. Coffee is much stronger than tea.
13. I need to wash down food with a drink.

Do You Have a Name Sign?

Most deaf people have name signs. These are simple signs that replace fingerspelling their names. For example, Connor's name sign is made by holding the letter C to her chin, where girl signs are usually made. Try the following tips to make up your own name sign:

Initial—Use the first letter of your name and place it in the girl or boy area.

Trait—Use the first letter of your name along with a special trait, such as long hair.

Existing sign—If your name already has a sign, you can use it for your name sign, such as "Candy."

CHAPTER 7

Home Signs

To help you remember the home signs, try to imagine the meaning behind each sign. For example, the word for *door* is signed by moving your hand as if you're opening and shutting a "door," while the sign for *window* is a hand that "raises" a "window."

Did You Know?

A hearing person without a TTY can call a deaf person, and vice versa, using the Relay System. By dialing a special 800 number, a hearing person will reach an operator with a TTY, who will interpret the conversation for both parties. She'll use a TTY to communicate with the deaf person and voice to communicate with the hearing person.

home

Touch flat *O* against mouth,
then cheek.

house

Shape roof with hands.

window

Rest *B* on top side of *B*;
open "window."

door

Make two *B*s side by side; open "door."

room

Shape room with flat hand.

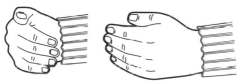

kitchen

Shake *K*.

Signing Space and Direction

Always sign toward the person you're talking to, using a relaxed hand and position. Make the signs in an imaginary square in front of your body, between your head and your waist. And don't forget to speak when you sign to a deaf person. (If you're practicing with another hearing person, don't speak so you can learn to read one another's signs.)

Try the following sentences using fingerspelling and signs:
1. What's the difference between your home and my home?
2. Does your house have three bedrooms or four?
3. It's hot. Will you please open the window?
4. You forgot to close the door!
5. Which room is your favorite?
6. I'm hungry. Where's the kitchen?
7. Does this building have a bathroom?
8. Are you hiding under your bed?
9. Come to the table. It's time for dinner.
10. Pull up a chair and rest your feet.
11. Do you have a desk for your homework?
12. I need to check my hair in a mirror.
13. How come your refrigerator has no food?

chair

Place *H* on top of *H*, both face down.

mirror

Hold up flat hand inward; move toward face.

refrigerator

Make two *R*s facing each other and shake.

Signing Space and Direction

Always sign toward the person you're talking to, using a relaxed hand and position. Make the signs in an imaginary square in front of your body, between your head and your waist. And don't forget to speak when you sign to a deaf person. (If you're practicing with another hearing person, don't speak so you can learn to read one another's signs.)

Try the following sentences using fingerspelling and signs:

1. What's the difference between your home and my home?
2. Does your house have three bedrooms or four?
3. It's hot. Will you please open the window?
4. You forgot to close the door!
5. Which room is your favorite?
6. I'm hungry. Where's the kitchen?
7. Does this building have a bathroom?
8. Are you hiding under your bed?
9. Come to the table. It's time for dinner.
10. Pull up a chair and rest your feet.
11. Do you have a desk for your homework?
12. I need to check my hair in a mirror.
13. How come your refrigerator has no food?

CHAPTER 8
Clothing Signs

Many of the clothes signs are more like gestures, because you act out putting on the clothing items. For example, "pants" is simply a gesture for pulling on your pants, while "hat" is a tap on the head. Can you guess ahead of time what the sign for each article of clothing will be?

Did You Know?

Several different kinds of hearing aids are available today. Deaf people used to wear "body aids," which were worn on the chest and attached to the ear. Today, most deaf people with hearing aids wear "behind-the-ear" aids or "in-the-ear" aids, which are nearly invisible.

shirt

Pull at shirt with *F*.

pants

Gesture pulling up pants.

coat/jacket

Act out putting on a coat.

hat

Tap top of head.

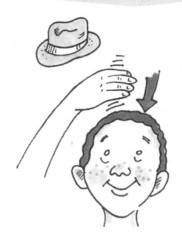

shoes

Tap *A*s side by side.

socks

Brush *1*s up and down.

pajamas

Sign *P* and *J*.

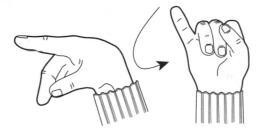

clothes

Brush down front with 5s.

Try the following sentences using fingerspelling or signs:
1. You look nice in your new shirt.
2. Did you forget to put on your pants?
3. It's cold outside, so wear your coat.
4. What kind of baseball hat do you like?
5. I like your new athletic shoes.
6. You always wear socks with little animals.
7. You can't wear your pajamas to school—can you?
8. Where do you buy most of your clothes?

What Is Body Language?

When using signs, be sure to express the meaning of your words through your body language and facial expression. For example, if you say "I (am) happy!" then you should relax, smile, and look pleasant.

CHAPTER 9
Color Signs

Most of the colors are signed using the first letter of the color. Shake or wave the sign in the air as shown below. Only a few color signs are different, and we've got tips to help you remember them. Can you sign your favorite color?

Did You Know?

Deaf people don't have superhuman powers when it comes to reading lips or seeing things that hearing people don't see. But without noise to distract them, they use their remaining senses more often and more efficiently.

red

Brush *1* across chin.

orange

Squeeze "orange" with *O* at mouth.

yellow

Shake *Y*.

green

Shake *G*.

blue

Shake *B*.

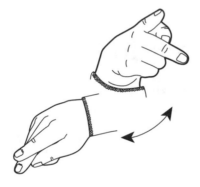

purple

Shake *P*.

white

Pull open hand to flat *O*
at chest.

black

Wipe *1* across forehead.

pink

Brush chin with *P*.

brown

Move *B* down side of face.

color

Wiggle four fingers on chin.

Try the following sentences using fingerspelling or signs:

1. My favorite flowers are red roses.
2. I look great when I wear orange.
3. Don't you think yellow is a happy color?
4. I'm going to turn my hair green on Halloween.
5. Are you driving a new blue car?
6. My new shirt is purple and has pineapples.
7. You look as white as a ghost!
8. I have an outfit that's all black.
9. Thanks for the stuffed pink pig.
10. If you mix too many colors, the picture will turn brown.

When Do You Point?

If a person, object, place, or even a color is nearby or visible, you can just point to it or point in the general direction of it. If the object is not present, use the sign first, and then you can point to a spot in space, as if it's there.

CHAPTER 10
Sport Signs

Signs for sports are easy to learn and easy to read, because they look like the action they represent. Just keep in mind that your hands will often substitute for your feet when gesturing a sport sign that involves feet. For other sport signs not listed, try imitating the action of the sport. You'll probably be close to the real sign.

Did You Know?

Instead of clapping to let a performer know what a good job they did, deaf people wave their hands in the air. That way the performers can see the "visible applause."

bike

Rotate "pedals" with hands.

swim

Imitate swimming.

baseball

Imitate swinging a baseball bat.

basketball

Imitate tossing a basketball.

football

Open fingers interlaced like a football.

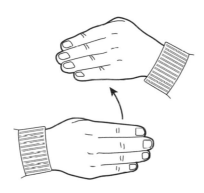

soccer

Kick *B* underneath *B*.

skating

Slide two bent *V*s back and forth, face up.

horseback riding

Sit upside-down *V* on side
of *B*; bounce.

sports

Move two fists back and
forth.

game

Make two fists come
together.

Try the following sentences using fingerspelling or signs:

1. I like to ride my bike to school.
2. Swimming is good for your health.
3. We play baseball at recess.
4. I'm the best basketball player on the team.
5. Our school football team is going to win.
6. The soccer team will practice on Saturday.
7. Do you have in-line skates?
8. I want to go horseback riding tomorrow.
9. I'm pretty good at sports.
10. Who's going to win the game today?

CHAPTER 11
Activity Signs

Which of the following activities is your favorite? Now that you're learning sign language, you've got a new activity—signing! Can you figure out how these signs came about just by trying them?

Did You Know?

Even though many deaf people can't hear music, they enjoy dancing just as much as hearing people. They can feel the beat of the music through the floor and dance right along with the crowd.

art

Draw / down palm.

photography

C at eye moves to C in palm.

drive

Imitate steering the car.

sign

Make *Ls* circle each other.

video

Shake *V* on back of hand.

movie

Wave *5* on back of hand.

radio

Circle *R* at ear.

TV

Sign *T* and *V*.

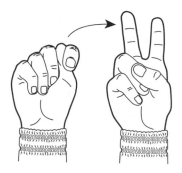

dance

Swing upside-down *V* over open palm.

music

Wave open flat hand over other arm.

birthday

Place flat hand on tummy; move out to open hand.

party

Shake *Ps*.

activity

Move two Cs back and forth in front of chest.

play

Twist *Ys* in air.

What Are Devices for the Deaf?

Deaf people often use devices to help them "hear," such as TV captioning, crying baby flashers, doorbell lights, telephone teletypewriters, and bed shakers. Some deaf people have "signal dogs" or "hearing ear dogs" that alert them to various sounds.

Try the following sentences using fingerspelling or signs:

1. I can do art on the computer.
2. Did you take photography in school?
3. We're going to drive to the park.
4. I'm learning to sign.

5. Do you like to watch videos?
6. What's your favorite scary movie?
7. Turn down the radio. It's too loud.
8. Turn off the TV and go outside.
9. Do you know any of the new dances?
10. I usually buy pop and rap music.
11. What are your favorite activities?
12. It's fun to play after school.

CHAPTER 12
Thought Signs

Although sign language is like talking without saying anything out loud, it's not mind reading! Your friends can't read your thoughts—unless you sign them. Here are some basic words to help you "think" with your hands.

Did You Know?

Deaf people drive cars, get married, have children, work in regular jobs, and do just about anything a hearing person can do. Can you think of something a deaf person can't do that a hearing person can—except maybe sing on key?

think

Point to forehead with *1*.

smart

Touch forehead with middle finger; twist outward.

dream

Wiggle *1* up from side of forehead.

forget

Wipe open hand to closed across forehead.

understand

Flick *1* up at forehead.

dumb

Tap forehead with *A*.

please

Circle tummy with flat hand.

thank you

Touch lips with fingertips
of flat hand; move out.

fine

Touch chest twice with
thumb of 5.

okay

Sign *O* and *K*.

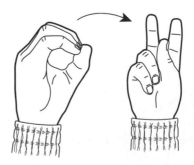

yes

Make *S* nod like head.

no

Make *U* touch thumb twice.

Hey, You!

How do you get the attention of a deaf person without being rude? If it's a hearing person, you say, "Excuse me." But if you're deaf, you have a few choices to attract attention. You can wave your hand, tap the person, or raise a hand as if you're ready to sign and wait for eye contact from the deaf person.

Try the following sentences using fingerspelling or signs:

1. I think I'm going to get an A on my paper.
2. You're pretty smart in math.
3. I had a dream about you last night.
4. Did you forget to bring your lunch?
5. It was dumb to take the test without studying.
6. I just don't understand my science teacher.
7. Please pass me the salt.
8. Thank you for helping me with my problem.
9. I'm feeling fine today.
10. Are you okay, or do you feel sick?
11. Yes, you may have some of my lunch.
12. No, you can't come in here.

CHAPTER 13
Feeling Signs

It's important to show how you feel by using facial expressions and body language that add meaning to the words. Hearing people use their voices to emphasize words, by speaking louder and softer. Deaf people do the same, using their faces to show emotions behind the words.

Did You Know?

Deaf people used to be discriminated against when they tried to get equal jobs, but the American Disabilities Act now prevents job discrimination. Deaf people can be just about anything—doctors, dentists, real estate agents, professors, reporters, and so on—if they have the proper education, training, and skills.

happy

Brush open hands
up chest twice.

sad

Move open hands down
face.

love

Cross arms at chest.

hate

Flick middle fingers out.

mad

"Scratch" face with claw.

afraid

Move *As* open to *5s* from sides to center of chest.

kiss

Touch fingertips to chin and cheek.

flirt

Touch thumbs of 5 together; wiggle fingers.

bad

Touch lips with fingertips; twist around and down.

good

Touch lips with fingertips;
move down to open hand.

surprise

Flick index fingers up
at temples.

sorry

Make fist circle chest.

tired

Touch fingertips to chest; bend hands downward.

sick

Place one middle finger on forehead, one on stomach.

like

Pull index and middle fingers out from chest.

feeling

Brush middle finger
up chest.

What If There's More Than One?

Here are some ways you can show plurals and multiples.

1. Repeat the sign several times, such as "fish, fish, fish."
2. Add the word "many," such as "There were many fish."
3. Add a number to the sign, such as "There were five fish."
4. Point to imaginary fish in space to show the number of fish.

Try the following sentences using fingerspelling and signs:
1. I'm so happy you found your cat.
2. Why are you sad today?
3. I love the bike I got for my birthday.
4. I don't mind vegetables, but I hate spinach!
5. Did your teacher get mad at you for being late?
6. Are you afraid of the dark?
7. I always kiss my parents good night.
8. Were you flirting with my friend?
9. I think you have a good idea.
10. Every time I do something bad I get in trouble.
11. I'm surprised to find you here.
12. I'm sorry you're sick.
13. Are you too tired to play baseball?
14. I like my best friend because she's nice.
15. I get the feeling you want to go home.

CHAPTER 14
Action Signs

Action signs are very animated. They incorporate movement to show what's happening, and they're signed with matching facial expression and body language. So put some energy into your signs and "show" people what you mean.

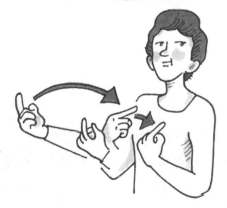

come

Pull index fingers toward you.

go

Move index fingers
outward.

walk

Make two fingers "walk."

run

Make thumbs touch; wiggle
index fingers, move forward.

jump

Make upside-down *V* jump and bend.

fall

Make upside-down *V* fall over.

throw

"Throw" flat *O* to open hand.

catch

Make open hands close to fists, one on top of the other.

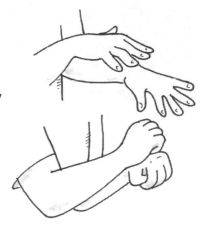

cook

Place palms together; flip top hand over.

telephone

Make Y pick up "telephone;" bring to ear.

talk

Move four fingers forward and back at mouth.

fast

Flick thumb out from bent index finger.

work

Tap one fist on top of other fist.

sleep

Open hand in front of face;
close to flat *O*.

look

Make *V* "look" from side of
eyes.

do/action

Place two *C*s face down;
move back and forth.

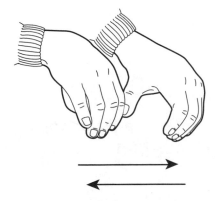

stop

Move side of flat hand
down on open palm.

hurry

Bounce *H*s up and down.

Try the following sentences using signs and fingerspelling:

1. Come over and we'll go to the store.
2. You should walk around the pool, not run.
3. If you jump on the bed, you might fall off.
4. You catch the ball when I throw it.
5. Telephone for pizza so I don't have to cook.
6. You talk too fast to interpret.

7. Do you ever sleep during work?
8. Look at the way you do your homework.
9. Stop running around in such a hurry!

What Is Total Communication?

Some deaf children are "oral," which means they use speech and speechreading (lipreading) to communicate. Other deaf children use only sign language to talk with one another. But many deaf children use total communication: They use all forms of communication, including gestures, sign, speech, speechreading, and amplification (hearing aids).

CHAPTER 15
Body Signs

Most of the body signs are easy to remember because you simply point to the part of body you're referring to. A couple of signs have been created to represent body parts when you can't point, so don't forget to learn those signs, too.

Did You Know?

It's easy to stop "listening" to someone when you're deaf. You just close your eyes.

body

Touch flat hands to upper chest, then lower chest.

person

Move *P*s down sides.

head

Touch bent hand to temple, then chin.

face

Circle face with index finger.

eyes

Point to each eye with index finger .

nose

Touch nose with index finger.

mouth

Touch mouth with index finger.

hair

Make *F* pull at hair.

hands

Slide side of hand down side of other; reverse.

feet

Point to feet with index finger.

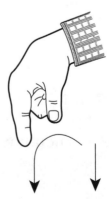

heart

Touch middle finger twice
to chest.

back

Touch back of shoulder.

Try the following sentences using sign language and fingerspelling:
1. These body signs are easy to remember.
2. What kind of a person are you?
3. Did you nod your head at the teacher?
4. You have a beautiful face.
5. What color are your eyes?
6. What happened to your nose?

7. Don't open your mouth during the movie.
8. You grew your hair long this summer.
9. Did you shake hands with that woman?
10. Your feet look good in those shoes.
11. Scary movies make my heart stop!
12. My back itches. Will you scratch it?

Turn the Body Sign into a Person . . .

The body sign comes in handy when you want to turn a regular sign into a person sign. For example, if you sign the word art and then add the "body" sign, you've got the word *artist.* Try turning the following signs into people: "cook," "swim," "dance," and "photography." Can you think of some other signs to create?

CHAPTER 16
School Signs

Since you spend much of your time in school, you'll need these school signs to use in class. But your sign language homework is fun. Just practice the signs and sentences here, and you'll be first in your class.

Did You Know?

In the past, deaf children at some "oral" schools were not allowed to use sign language and were punished when they signed. The schools believed that if they used sign language, they would not learn to speak.

school

Clap your hands.

teacher

Move flat Os out from forehead; plus *body* sign.

class

Move two Cs from chest outward in a circle.

learn

Make claw hand in palm; pull to flat *O* at forehead.

study

Wiggle open hand at palm.

student

Make *learn* plus *body* sign.

library

Make *L* in a small circle.

book

Place palms together;
open "book."

read

Swipe *V* down across open
palm.

write

"Write" on open palm.

computer

Tap C on forehead.

paper

Open palms, facing
opposite ways; tap.

homework

Touch flat *O* to cheek, plus
sign for *work*.

recess

Shake two *R*s.

Sign Language Helps Everyone

Learning and using sign language can help improve the skills of hearing kids as well as deaf children. Sign language can help increase language development, reading skills, vocabulary, and visual memory. So while you practice signing, you're developing all kinds of important skills.

Try the following sentences using sign language and fingerspelling:

1. What school do you go to?
2. I think I know who your teacher is.
3. My sign language class is my favorite.
4. Where did you learn to sign?
5. Let's study fingerspelling together.
6. Are you a student in Mrs. Warner's class?
7. I want to go to school in California.
8. The library is closed on Sunday.
9. What book do you want to read for class?
10. Write your name on my notebook.
11. Do you know how to use the computer?
12. I have to write a paper about American history.
13. Did you finish your homework?
14. Let's meet at recess to practice signing.

CHAPTER 17
Calendar Signs

Signs that represent time, days, and weather are easy to learn once you learn the patterns. See whether you can figure out how the following groups of signs are similar and how they change slightly. You'll soon be able to sign any time of day, any day of the year.

Did You Know?

In the 1960s, educators found that when a deaf child used all forms of communication, including speech, signs, gestures, lipreading, and hearing aids, that student learned language more efficiently.

year

Set fist on other fist;
circle around.

week

Place index finger on palm;
swipe across.

day

Set elbow on fingertips;
move *D* hand down flat.

yesterday

Touch *Y* to cheek, then back to jaw.

today

Set *Y*s face up; move down.

tomorrow

Move *A* forward at side of head.

time

Touch back of wrist with index finger.

morning

Place hand at inside elbow, extend arm, raise.

noon

Place arm straight up, rest elbow on back of hand.

night

Rest cupped hand on back of hand.

Sunday

Open hands face out; make circle.

Monday

Circle *M*.

Tuesday

Circle *T*.

Wednesday

Circle *W*.

Thursday

Circle *H*.

Friday

Circle *F*.

Saturday

Circle *S*.

rain

Wave open hands down.

snow

Make open fingers flutter down.

sun

Tap C on eye.

Try the following sentences using sign language and fingerspelling:

1. What year were you born?
2. I forgot my lunch last week.
3. This is a special day for me.
4. Yesterday was my birthday.
5. Today is the last day of the month.
6. Tomorrow there is no school.

7. What time do you want to meet for lunch?
8. I have to go to the doctor in the morning.
9. The game will be played at noon.
10. I'm having a slumber party at night.
11. Sunday is the day I like to rest.
12. Monday is the first day of school.
13. I get to go to dance class on Tuesday.
14. Is Wednesday your favorite day of the week?
15. Thursday night is a good TV night.
16. Thank goodness it's Friday!
17. Saturday is the best day of the week.
18. I hope it doesn't rain at the wedding.
19. It doesn't snow where I live.
20. I wish the sun would come out.

Past, Present, or Future?

Many signs that represent the past move backward, while many future signs move forward. For example, if you want to sign "next week," move your index finger forward when signing "week," and move it backward if you want to sign "last week."

CHAPTER 18
Silly and Fun Signs

You've learned lots of basic signs, so now it's time to learn some silly and fun signs. Here are a few to get you started, so you can talk about stinky monsters, ugly ghosts, and funny fools!

Did You Know?

The terms *deaf and dumb* and *deaf mute* are no longer accepted by the Deaf community. Deaf people are not "dumb" or "mute"—they have vocal cords. Some just choose not to verbalize. And of course, they aren't "dumb" in the other sense of the word. They're just as smart as hearing people.

awful

Flick middle fingers to
open hands.

ugly

Pull *X* across your nose.

cute

Brush *U* across chin.

hot

Twist claw hand from
mouth outward.

dirty

Place hand under chin,
wiggle fingers.

stink

Pinch nose.

ghost

Pull *F*s apart and wiggle.

monster

Claw hands near temples.

bored

Place index finger on
side of nose; twist.

fool

Move *Y* across face.

secret

Place thumb of *A* on lower lip.

lie

Brush chin with flat hand.

tease

Stick out index and baby fingers; jab forward.

laugh

Swipe index fingers upward at mouth.

delicious / favorite

Touch chin twice with middle finger.

sweet

Brush chin with fingertips of *B*.

silly

Wiggle *Y* in front of face.

funny

Brush nose twice with *U*.

Do Hearing People Sign the Same as Deaf People?

Hearing people often use signed English, which means they use ASL signs in English word order. Deaf people use ASL signs, as well as ASL sentence structure, grammar, and syntax. Luckily, most deaf people can understand signed English. Several other forms of sign language are used in the United States, such as SEE signs, Pidgin Sign English, and Cued Speech. Sign language is used in other countries, such as British Sign Language, but the vocabulary is often different.

Try the following sentences using sign language and fingerspelling:
1. That was an awful movie last night!
2. This outfit looks ugly.
3. Chris is so cute!
4. That guy is hot!
5. I got dirty when I fell in the mud.
6. It stinks in here!
7. I'm not afraid of ghosts.
8. Is there a monster under the bed?
9. Do you ever get bored sometimes?
10. What kind of fool do you think I am?

11. I have a secret and I won't tell!
12. Did you ever tell a lie?
13. Don't tease your brother!
14. Did you laugh during the movie?
15. My favorite ice cream is chocolate. It's delicious!
16. My new bike is sweet!
17. Stop being so silly!
18. I love to use the funny signs.

CHAPTER 19
Sign Language Games and Activities

Now that you've learned lots of signs and you've practiced until you know them by heart, it's time to play some sign language games. Gather your friends who are also learning to sign and have some fun with ASL!

Here you'll find over forty sign language games, along with more than 40 bonus games. Check the "Number of Players" to find out whether you can play alone or need other players. The "Sign Level" will help you match your signing ability to the game—beginner, intermediate, or advanced. "Must Know" tells you whether you need fingerspelling or signs or both. Gather the "Materials Needed" before you begin playing, then read over "How to Play" so you know the rules. The "Bonus Play" offers another way to play the game, to help build your skills and extend

Did You Know?

If a deaf person is trying to lipread a number of hearing people engaged in conversation, it may be difficult to keep track of the moving discussion. Take a moment before speaking, so the deaf person can keep up, and check to make sure he or she is following along.

the fun. Under "Teacher Tips," instructors will find ways to play the games in the classroom.

Are your hands warmed up? Fingers limber? Brain engaged? Ready, set, go play some sign language games!

Add-a-Sign

If you've been practicing the manual alphabet, you can play Add-a-Sign.

NUMBER OF PLAYERS: TWO OR MORE
SIGN LEVEL: BEGINNER
MUST KNOW: FINGERSPELLING

Materials needed
- Pad and pencil

How to play
1. Choose a category, such as "Flowers," "Candy Bars," "Furniture," "States," "Fast-Food Restaurants," "Clothing," "School Subjects," and so on.

2. One player begins the game by signing or fingerspelling a word in the selected category, that begins with the first letter of the alphabet, *A*. For example, if the category is "Candy Bars," the first player might fingerspell, "Almond Joy."

3. The next player must sign a category word beginning with the next letter of the alphabet, *B*, such as "Butterfinger."

4. The game continues until the alphabet is complete.

5. If a player cannot sign or fingerspell a word in the category beginning with the next letter, she must pass to the next player and lose a point.

6. If that next player can sign a word that begins with the letter, he gets a bonus point.

7. The player with the most points wins the game.

Bonus Play

• Instead of going through the alphabet in order, photocopy the manual alphabet, cut up the letters individually, mix them up, and stack them face down. Each player must pick the top card, read the manual letter, and fingerspell an item from the category using that letter.

Teacher Tip

• Divide the class up into groups of three or four, and have them play the game.

• Have the kids use school topics or their spelling words as categories.

Alphasign

You'll be surprised how many signs use letters of the alphabet.

NUMBER OF PLAYERS: TWO OR MORE

SIGN LEVEL: INTERMEDIATE

MUST KNOW: FINGERSPELLING AND SOME SIGNS

Materials needed
- Pad and pencil

How to play
1. One player begins the game by signing a word, using the first let-ter of the alphabet, *A*. For example, she might sign the word *girl*, which uses the letter *A* stroking the side of the face.

2. The next player must sign a word using the next letter of the alphabet, *B*. For example, he might sign the word *back*, moving the letter *B* toward the back.

3. The game continues until the alphabet is complete.

4. If a player can't think of a sign using the next alphabet letter, the next player gets a chance. If he can sign a word, he gets a point.

5. Play moves on to the next player and continues through the alphabet.

6. The player with the most points wins the game.

Bonus play
- Instead of moving onto the next letter, see how many signs you can come up with using the letter *A*. When everyone is stuck, move onto the next letter.

Teacher tip
- Break the class up into groups of three or four and play the game.

Blind Spot

Helen Keller learned to sign, even though she was not only deaf but also blind. Try your hand at it, the way Helen Keller did.

NUMBER OF PLAYERS: 2

SIGN LEVEL: BEGINNER

MUST KNOW: FINGERSPELLING

Materials needed

- Paper and pencil
- Clean hands!

How to play

1. One player writes down a short sentence without letting the other player see it.

2. A second player closes her eyes.

3. The first player places his hand in the other player's hand and slowly spells the first word of the sentence.

4. The second player must nod when she understands the word or shake her head if she doesn't, then the first player must repeat it.

5. When the sentence is complete, the second player must say the sentence out loud.

6. Players take turns fingerspelling sentences in one another's hands.

Bonus play

- Both close your eyes and have a conversation back and forth, by fingerspelling in one another's hands.

Teacher tip

- Divide the class into teams of six or eight (equal numbers in the teams), and have them pass words down the row like a relay race. See which team finishes first—with the correct sentence.

Crazy Categories

How many items can you sign in one category?

NUMBER OF PLAYERS: 2 OR MORE, IN PAIRS

SIGN LEVEL: ADVANCED

MUST KNOW: FINGERSPELLING AND MOST OF THE SIGNS IN THE BOOK

Materials needed

- Pencil and paper for each pair
- One-minute timer

How to play

1. Have pairs sit facing each other.

2. Choose a category, such as "animals," "fruits and vegetables," "clothing," "desserts," "school subjects," "sports," "TV shows," "musical groups," "pizza toppings," "fast-food restaurants," "drinks," and so on.

3. Set a timer or stop watch for one minute.

4. One player fingerspells as many words in the category as she can to her partner, while her partner writes them down. (Don't forget to keep your eyes on the fingerspelling, not on the paper!)

5. At the end of one minute, the game stops.

6. Add up the number of category items and write down the total.

7. Reverse the play, so that the person who signed is now the reader, and the person who read the signs is now the signer.

8. Continue taking turns and adding up points.

9. The player or players with the most points wins the game.

Bonus play
- Restrict the game to only fingerspelling or only signs, to make the game more challenging, and help increase those skills.

Teacher tip
- Divide the class into pairs and see which pair comes up with the most correct answers. If there's an extra player, you can be her partner.
- Use school subjects for the categories.

Daffy Deaf-initions

How's your sign language vocabulary? Find out with a game of Daffy Deaf-initions.

NUMBER OF PLAYERS: 2 OR MORE
SIGN LEVEL: BEGINNER
MUST KNOW: FINGERSPELLING

Materials needed
- Paper and pencil

How to play

1. One player creates a sign that represents a word, making it as close to the concept of the word as possible. For example, the player might make up a sign for the word "danger" by crashing his fists together or combining two signs, such as *stop* and *afraid*.

2. Have the other player use fingerspelling to guess what the new made-up sign means.

3. Take turns making up new signs and guessing their meanings.

4. Keep score to see who can guess the most signs.

Bonus play

• Act out sentences instead of just words, without using signs.

Teacher tip

• Break into groups of three or four.
• Have the players act out information from their lessons or spelling words.

Decode the Code

Can you translate the following sentences from the manual alphabet?

NUMBER OF PLAYERS: 1 OR MORE

SIGN LEVEL: BEGINNER

MUST KNOW: FINGERSPELLING

Materials needed
• Pencil

How to play
1. Translate the manual letters below (see answers at end of chapter):

1.

2.

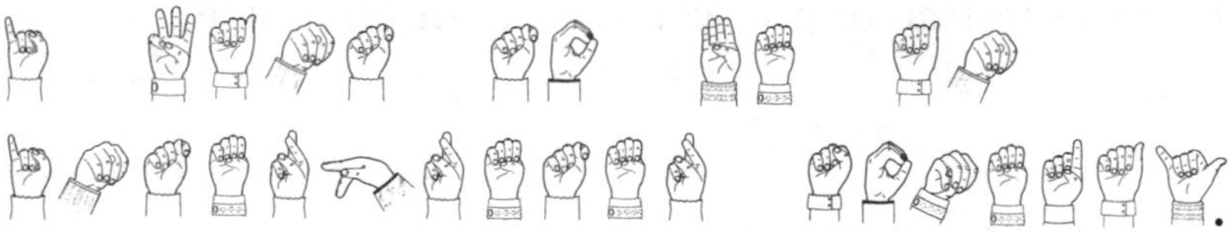

3.

4.

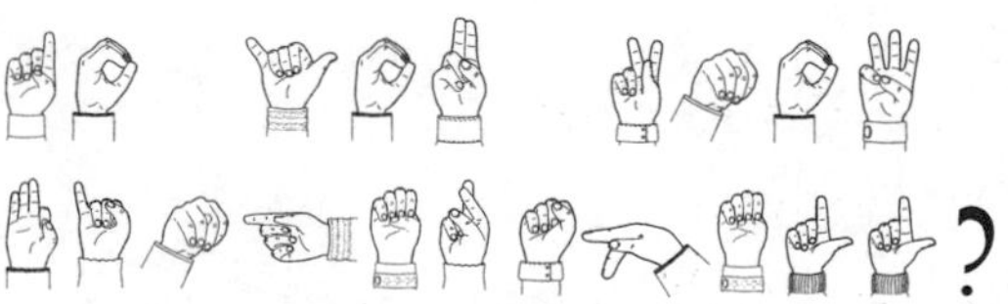

5.

6.

7.

8.

9.

10.

Bonus play
- Make up your own sentences for a friend, by drawing the manual alphabet on paper and having her translate it.
- Practice drawing the manual alphabet letters, then write your name on a T-shirt in manual letters, using puffy paints.

Teacher tip
- Reproduce the game above for all your students, and have them translate the manual alphabet. Then have the students create their own, pass them around, and let the other students translate them.

Face Your Feelings

Can people read your face as well as your signs?

NUMBER OF PLAYERS: 2 OR MORE

SIGN LEVEL: BEGINNER

MUST KNOW: FACIAL EXPRESSIONS

silly	angry	ponder
happy	disgusted	horrified

Materials needed

- Paper and pencil

How to play

1. One player chooses a facial expression from the illustrations above without telling her partner which one it is.

2. That player must imitate the facial expressions.

3. The second player must try to guess which face the first player is expressing.

4. Players take turns making faces and guessing the feelings expressed.

Bonus play
- Make up your own facial expressions to express other feelings.
- Try expressing the sentence "Sit down," in ten different ways, using facial expressions to give the sentence different meanings.

Teacher tip
- Have the kids take turns coming to the front of the class to demonstrate an assigned emotion through facial expressions.
- Have them use body language to express additional emotions.

Footloose

You can talk with your hands, but can you talk with your feet?

NUMBER OF PLAYERS: 2 OR MORE

SIGN LEVEL: BEGINNER

MUST KNOW: SOME SIGNS

Materials needed
- Paper and pencil

How to play

1. Players write down movie titles, song titles, or book titles and put them in a hat or bowl.

2. The first player picks a title to sign or act out—with his feet!

3. See if the other players can tell what that player is trying to express.

4. Keep score to see who has the most expressive feet!

Bonus play

- Keep score with your feet, too!

Teacher tip

- You better play this game outside!

Funny Fingerspelling

Use the comics to practice your fingerspelling and have a laugh!

NUMBER OF PLAYERS: 2 OR MORE

SIGN LEVEL: INTERMEDIATE

MUST KNOW: FINGERSPELLING AND SOME SIGNS

Materials needed

- Funny pages
- Paper and pencil

How to play

1. Cut out comic strips from the funny papers.

2. Each player chooses a strip and writes down the words on a separate sheet of paper. (Don't let anyone see your paper.)

3. Black out the words on the strips.

4. Players sign the words to the strip and show the pictures to the other players as they sign. They must read the signs to understand the comic strip.

5. Check to see if everyone understands the joke!

Bonus play
- Instead of letting the other players see the comic drawings, sign the strip and describe or act out the action.

Teacher tip
- Break the class into groups of three or four, and have them sign and act out the strips for each other.

Ghost Fingers

If you know how to play the game Ghost, you'll have a ghost of a chance at winning Ghost Fingers.

NUMBER OF PLAYERS: 2 OR MORE

SIGN LEVEL: BEGINNER

MUST KNOW: FINGERSPELLING

Materials needed
- Pencil and paper

4. The second player who received the word gets to start the game. She must give a clue to her partner that is similar to the word, to help her partner guess the word. She might also give a word that means the opposite or that rhymes with the word. For example, if the word is smart, the player might fingerspell or sign a related word, such as brain or think. Or she might sign a word that means the opposite, such as stupid, or a word that rhymes, such as start. She cannot give a clue that has any part of the actual word in it, however.

5. The second player must try to guess the original word, using the clue. He can only guess one word.

6. If he cannot guess the word, the turn goes to the other team.

7. Continue guessing until the player gets the word correct.

8. Keep score to see which team wins.

Bonus play

- You can play the game with just two people, by keeping track of how many guesses it takes each player to guess the word. The player with the most points is the loser.

Teacher tip

- Divide the class into groups of four, with two-person teams. Prepare the words ahead of time, by writing them on index cards, using vocabulary words from your lessons or text.

Guess-Sign

Can you guess the sign, one word at a time? It's just like Password.

NUMBER OF PLAYERS: 4

SIGN LEVEL: INTERMEDIATE

MUST KNOW: FINGERSPELLING AND SOME SIGNS

Materials needed

- Paper and pencil
- Dictionary

How to play

1. Players divide into two-person teams.

2. The first player of one pair looks in the dictionary for a simple word that everyone knows.

3. He writes down the word on a piece of paper and passes it to one player on the other team to see. The remaining two players do not get to see the word.

Did You Know?

It's frustrating for a deaf person watching TV when suddenly the words "Special Bulletin" appear on the screen without captions. Deaf people have no idea what's happening and wonder if it's only a simple weather update or news of a nuclear explosion!

4. The second player who received the word gets to start the game. She must give a clue to her partner that is similar to the word, to help her partner guess the word. She might also give a word that means the opposite or that rhymes with the word. For example, if the word is smart, the player might fingerspell or sign a related word, such as brain or think. Or she might sign a word that means the opposite, such as stupid, or a word that rhymes, such as start. She cannot give a clue that has any part of the actual word in it, however.

5. The second player must try to guess the original word, using the clue. He can only guess one word.

6. If he cannot guess the word, the turn goes to the other team.

7. Continue guessing until the player gets the word correct.

8. Keep score to see which team wins.

Bonus play
• You can play the game with just two people, by keeping track of how many guesses it takes each player to guess the word. The player with the most points is the loser.

Teacher tip
• Divide the class into groups of four, with two-person teams. Prepare the words ahead of time, by writing them on index cards, using vocabulary words from your lessons or text.

Guess the Gesture

Do you recognize these familiar gestures?

NUMBER OF PLAYERS: 1 OR MORE

SIGN LEVEL: BEGINNER

MUST KNOW: UNIVERSAL SIGNS

Materials needed

- Paper and pencil

How to play

See if you can guess what the following gestures mean (see answers at end of chapter):

1. What does mean, besides the letter *V*?

2. What does mean, besides the letter *S*?

3. What does mean, besides the letter *F*?

4. What does mean?

5. What does mean?

6. What does mean?

7. What does mean?

8. What does mean?

9. What does mean?

Bonus play

- Make up your own universal signs and see if you can communicate with your partner. For example, what might be a universal

sign for "Where is . . . ?"; "Sit down"; "Who are you?"; "I'm hungry"; "Where's the bathroom?"; "You're cute"?
- Watch for universal signs throughout the day and see how many you notice. (Watch out for those bad ones!)

Teacher tip
- Demonstrate the signs for the class, and have them guess what they mean.
- Collect more universal signs from other countries and discuss how they're similar and different to the gestures in our culture.

Hand-y Map

You don't need a map when you keep your hands handy!

NUMBER OF PLAYERS: 2 OR MORE

SIGN LEVEL: BEGINNER

MUST KNOW: DIRECTION

Materials needed
- Paper and pencil

How to play
1. One player hides an object somewhere in the house or yard.

2. He draws a map to the object without letting the other players see it.

3. That player must direct another player to the object, using only his hands to guide her. He can show her where to go, a little at a

time, by using his hands to make the other player turn, go a certain direction, stop, and so on. Remember, he can only use his hands to guide the other player.

4. Players take turns leading each one another to hidden objects, using only hands to guide them.

Bonus play
- When you get really good at the game, try giving the directions ahead of time—all at once—then see if the other player can find the hidden object by remembering the hand directions.

Teacher tip
- Make up maps to lead the kids around the school grounds. Break the students up into two-person teams, and have one player "show" the other player where to go, using only his hands. See who can find the hidden object first, or time the teams to see who finds it the fastest.

Laughing Fingers

Show your sense of humor in sign language.

NUMBER OF PLAYERS: 2 OR MORE

SIGN LEVEL: ADVANCED

MUST KNOW: FINGERSPELLING AND MOST SIGNS FROM THE BOOK

Materials needed
- Joke book

How to play

1. Get a joke book from the library or bookstore, or have players make up their own jokes.

2. Have players read or tell jokes to one another in sign language.

3. If the other players laugh at the jokes, that means they must have understood them!

4. If they don't laugh, they either don't understand the signs or the joke—or maybe it's just not funny!

Bonus play

- Tell "Knock-Knock" jokes to engage both players in the game.
- "Laugh" in sign language by quickly fingerspelling the letters, "h-a-h-a-h-a." Just bend the letter *H* into the letter *A*, several times. If it's really funny, spell "Ha" with both hands.

Teacher tip

- Let the kids take turns coming to the front of the class to tell a joke.
- Tell a joke to the students in sign language every day before you start the lesson.

Letter Out

Challenge your fingerspelling and signs when you have to watch for the "Letter Out."

NUMBER OF PLAYERS: 2 OR MORE

SIGN LEVEL: INTERMEDIATE

MUST KNOW: FINGERSPELLING AND SOME SIGNS

Materials needed

- Paper and pencil

How to play

1. Players first decide on a topic for conversation, such as "What happened at school today," "Plans for tomorrow," "Favorite movies," and so on.

2. One player chooses a letter of the alphabet and writes it down.

3. Players must have a conversation back and forth in sign language and fingerspelling, without using the selected alphabet letter. For example, if the selected letter is *N*, players can't use that letter. If someone signs, "Today at school I met a friend," the *N* in "friend" would cost that player a point. He would have to use the word *pal*, *kid*, or some other word that doesn't have an *N*.

4. If a player accidentally uses the letter, she loses a point.

5. The player with the most points loses the game.

Bonus play

- Make the game even harder by choosing two letters you can't use.

Teacher tip

- Divide the class into groups of four or five, and have them take turns discussing a lesson with a missing letter.

Lip Service

*Lipreading looks easy in the movies, but try it yourself
and find out how hard it really is.*

NUMBER OF PLAYERS: 1 OR MORE

SIGN LEVEL: BEGINNER

MUST KNOW: SOME LIPREADING

Materials needed

- Television

How to play

1. Players choose a TV show where the people are talking clearly, such as a newscast or talk show.

2. Turn off the sound.

3. Players must try to lipread what the people are saying.

4. Ask one another how much was understood.

Bonus play

- Play a video instead of a TV show, and try to lipread it. Play back the video a second time to see how accurate your lipreading was.

Teacher tip

- Play a video with the sound down, and have two or three players take the parts of the different people on the screen. Have them try to lipread the speakers, out loud.

Match-a-Sign

How well do you know what your partner will sign?

NUMBER OF PLAYERS: 2 OR MORE

SIGN LEVEL: INTERMEDIATE

MUST KNOW: FINGERSPELLING AND SIGNS

Materials needed

- Paper and pencil

How to play

1. Choose a category, such as "trees," "foods," "ice cream flavors," "snacks," "dog breeds," and so on.

2. One player taps the table.

3. As soon as he does, all players sign or fingerspell one item from the selected category. For example, if the category is "trees," players might sign *oak, apple, elm*, and so on.

4. All players who match each other with the same item in the category get a point. For example, if two players both sign or fingerspell the word *oak*, they get a point.

5. Players keep changing categories and trying to match signs.

6. The player with the most points wins the game.

Bonus play

- Do the opposite and try to fingerspell or sign a word in the category that won't match the others. Award points for those who don't match.

Teacher tip

• Divide the class into groups of four or five. Include vocabulary words from your lessons as categories.

Mime in Time

You don't need speech or signs to express yourself
when you play Mime in Time.

NUMBER OF PLAYERS: 2 OR MORE

SIGN LEVEL: BEGINNER

MUST KNOW: HOW TO EXPRESS YOURSELF WITHOUT WORDS OR SIGNS

Materials needed

• Paper and pencil

How to play

1. One player thinks of a common phrase, such as "Happy birthday to you," "Keep an open mind," "Try, try, and you'll succeed," "Practice makes perfect," and so on.

2. Instead of signing or saying the phrase, that player must act it out for the other players.

3. The others must try to guess what the first player is miming.

4. Players take turns miming and guessing the phrases.

5. The first player to guess the phrase wins a point. The player with the most points wins the game.

Bonus play

- If you have four or more players, write down phrases ahead of time, then divide into teams and act out the phrases for the other team.

Teacher tip

- Write down phrases from students' literature, divide the students into four-person teams, and have them act out the phrases.

Missing Fingers

Can you still read the words when some letters are missing?
Just fill in the gaps and the words will appear.

NUMBER OF PLAYERS: 2 OR MORE

SIGN LEVEL: INTERMEDIATE

MUST KNOW: FINGERSPELLING

Materials needed

- Paper and pencil

How to play

1. One player picks a category, such as "movie titles," "stores," "book titles," "rock stars," and so on.

2. That player must write down a list of items from the selected category, such as *The Little Mermaid, Star Wars, Home Alone,* and so on, then strike out the vowels.

3. He must fingerspell a word or phrase from his selected category to the other players, leaving out the vowels. For example, if the category is "Movie Titles" and he has selected *The Little Mermaid,* he would cross off the vowels, leaving *T-H-L-T-T-L-M-R-M-D.*

4. The second player must try to read the word or phrase aloud. If she gets it right, she gets a point.

5. Take turns spelling words with missing vowels in various categories.

6. Count up points to determine the winner.

Bonus play

• If a player has trouble reading the fingerspelled phrases, let him write the letters down, then guess the phrase.

Teacher tip

• Divide students into small groups of three or four, then write down lines from students' literature or their spelling words, and have students fingerspell them without the vowels for others to guess.

Movie Signs

Would you recognize a movie just by the acting? It depends on the actor!

NUMBER OF PLAYERS: 2 OR MORE

SIGN LEVEL: BEGINNER

MUST KNOW: MOVIE SCENES

Materials needed

- Paper and pencil

How to play

1. Players must think of a favorite movie scene from a comedy, adventure, horror, science fiction, or animated film.

2. One player acts out the scene for the others. Don't use any signs or fingerspelling—that's cheating!

3. The other players must try to guess what movie it's from.

4. Keep track of points to see who wins.

Bonus play

- Act out several scenes by the same actor, and see whether the others can guess who you are.

Teacher tip

- Break the class into groups of five or six, and have them act out scenes from their lessons, history books, literature, or even spelling words. See whether the others can guess.

Name That Tune

Can you name that tune with only a few words of the song?

NUMBER OF PLAYERS: 2 OR MORE

SIGN LEVEL: INTERMEDIATE TO ADVANCED

MUST KNOW: FINGERSPELLING AND SIGNS

Materials needed
- Lines from favorite popular songs
- Paper and pencil

How to play
1. One player chooses a popular song.

2. She must sign and fingerspell a line from the song, moving her hand up and down to match the beat and rhythm of the song.

3. Have the next player try to guess the song.

4. If he can't guess the song, give him another line from the song.

5. Keep giving lines from the song until the player guesses it.

6. Players take turns signing and guessing songs.

7. Write down how many lines or words it takes before the other person guesses the song. The person with the most lines loses.

Bonus play
- Fingerspell or sign only one word from the song until the other person guesses. Record how many words it takes.

Teacher tip

• Instead of using song lyrics, recite lines from class readings, literature, or famous sayings.

Number Signs

If you know the numbers from 0 to 10, you'll be number one at this game.

NUMBER OF PLAYERS: 2 OR MORE

SIGN LEVEL: INTERMEDIATE

MUST KNOW: NUMBERS AND SOME SIGNS

Materials needed

• Paper and pencil

How to play

1. The first player must think of a sign that uses the number *0*. For example, she might sign *orange* or *teach*.

2. The second player must use the next number, *1*, in a sign. For example, he might sign *mouse* or *think*.

3. Players continue until they reach ten. Repeat until players can't think of any more signs using the numbers.

4. If a player can't think of another sign using a number, she gets a point.

5. The person with the most points loses.

Bonus play

- Remove the face cards from a deck of cards, shuffle them, and take turns choosing a card and making a sign using the number on the card.

Teacher tip

- Have a number bee, with all the students taking turns using the numbers to make a sign.

Oppo-Sign

Here's a twist on your favorite movie titles. Can you figure them out through the signs?

NUMBER OF PLAYERS: 2 OR MORE

SIGN LEVEL: INTERMEDIATE

MUST KNOW: FINGERSPELLING AND SOME SIGNS

Materials needed

- Paper and pencil
- List of movies

How to play

1. One player thinks of a movie title, such as *Star Wars* or *The Little Mermaid.*

2. Instead of signing the movie title, she must sign words that are the opposite or similar to the movie title words. For example, for *Star Wars*, she might fingerspell or sign "Moon Peace" or "planet

fights." For *The Little Mermaid*, she might sign "big fish" or "tiny shark."

3. The other player must try to guess the real movie title from the Oppo-signs.

4. Players take turns making up mixed-up movie titles and guessing the titles.

Bonus play

• Do the same with song titles, book titles, or common phrases.

Teacher tip

• Make up Oppo-Signs for school subjects, literary quotes, historical sites, or book titles and have the class write down the answers.

Rhyme 'n' Sign

Can you rhyme and sign at the same time? It's just like walking and chewing gum.

NUMBER OF PLAYERS: 2 OR MORE

SIGN LEVEL: INTERMEDIATE

MUST KNOW: FINGERSPELLING AND SOME SIGNS

Materials needed

• Paper and pencil

How to play

1. One player begins a rhyme by fingerspelling and signing a line. For example, she might sign, "Once upon a time . . ."

2. The next player must continue the rhyme by fingerspelling and signing a line that rhymes with the first line. For example, he might sign, "A boy found a dime . . ."

3. Players take turns continuing the rhyme, line by line.

4. If someone can't come up with a rhyming line, he gets a point and a new rhyme begins.

5. The person with the most points, loses the game.

Bonus play
- Take turns fingerspelling as many rhyming words as you can. The first person who can't sign a rhyme loses a point.

Teacher tip
- Use the class vocabulary words to rhyme.

Secret Code

Write your messages in the manual alphabet so no one else can read your secrets.

NUMBER OF PLAYERS: 2 OR MORE

SIGN LEVEL: BEGINNER

MUST KNOW: MANUAL ALPHABET

Materials needed
- Sign language font, such as Gallaudet. (You can buy the font or download it from the Internet. Go to 192.188.148.10/Education/fonts.html) Use your search engine to hunt for the words

"Gallaudet Font."
- Paper and pencil

How to play

1. Find a sign language font and load it onto your computer.

2. Type a message to a friend who knows fingerspelling, using an English font.

3. Check the spelling and grammar to make sure it's correct.

4. Translate the letter using your sign language font.

5. Give your letter to a friend to translate.

Bonus play

- Mail secret messages to friends who don't know sign language, with a photocopy of the manual alphabet, so they can translate it and learn the manual alphabet. As long as they have the code, they can translate the message!

Teacher tip

- Type up your lesson or spelling words using a sign language font, make copies for your students, and pass them out to translate.
- Let the students take turns typing up messages for the class.

Shape It

Can you shape the words to match the shape in the bag?

NUMBER OF PLAYERS: 3 OR MORE

SIGN LEVEL: BEGINNER

MUST KNOW: GESTURES

Materials needed

- Items with distinct shapes or textures, such as a sponge, a flower, a bar of soap, a candy bar, and so on.
- Bag

How to play

1. One player places something interesting in a bag without anyone seeing it.

2. The next player must feel what's inside the bag.

3. After he feels the object, he must try to describe it to the next player by shaping his hands. No sign language or fingerspelling allowed!

4. If the next player guesses it within three tries, she gets a point.

Bonus play

- Have the player act out the object instead of shaping it.

Teacher tip

- Divide the class into small groups of three or four, and have them take turns shaping objects in the bag for the other players.

Sign-a-Poem

Sign language is poetry in motion. See for yourself as your sign your favorite poems.

NUMBER OF PLAYERS: 2 OR MORE

SIGN LEVEL: INTERMEDIATE TO ADVANCED

MUST KNOW: FINGERSPELLING AND SIGNS

Materials needed

- Book of fun poems, such as Shel Silverstein's

How to play

1. Find a book of fun poems from the library or bookstore.

2. Have one player sign a poem while the next player reads the sign aloud.

Bonus play

- Act out the poem as you sign it, for a dramatic reading.
- Act out a play in sign language.

Teacher tip

- Have the students sign poems you are teaching in class. Have them practice enough to memorize the poems, then have them present the poems in class.
- Have the kids act out a short play.

Sign-a-Sketch

There are several ways to communicate besides speech and sign.
How about by sketching?

NUMBER OF PLAYERS: 2 OR MORE

SIGN LEVEL: BEGINNER

MUST KNOW: FINGERSPELLING

Materials needed
- Paper and pencil

How to play
1. One player takes a pencil and paper and begins to draw an object.

2. Each time she draws a line, she must look up at the other player to see whether he can guess what it is, using fingerspelling and sign language to ask questions.

3. Continue drawing and signing guesses until either the picture is finished or the player has guessed what it is.

4. Players take turns sketching and signing.

5. Write down how many seconds or minutes it takes each player to guess the answer. The player with the fewest minutes wins the game.

Bonus play
- If you have three or more players, have the players race each other to guess the answer.

Did You Know?

Today, most schools use bilingual/bicultural—called bi-bi—which recognizes British and American Sign Language as two different languages, equally valued.

Teacher tip
• Divide the group into three or four players. Have the students use spelling words, vocabulary words, or concepts from their lessons.

Sign-a-Story

How will your story end?

NUMBER OF PLAYERS: 2 OR MORE

SIGN LEVEL: BEGINNER

MUST KNOW: FINGERSPELLING

Materials needed
• Paper and pencil

How to play
1. One player begins a sentence by signing or fingerspelling one word.

2. The next player continues the story by repeating the first word and adding the next word, in sign.

3. Play continues until there is a complete sentence.

4. Have the player say it aloud to see how it turned out.

Bonus play
• When you get good at signing sentences word by word, start signing stories, sentence by sentence.

Teacher tip
• Divide the students into groups, and have them use spelling or vocabulary words in their sentences.

Signing the Obvious

Here's a game to play with friends who don't know sign language.

NUMBER OF PLAYERS: 2 OR MORE

SIGN LEVEL: BEGINNER

MUST KNOW: SOME EASY SIGNS

Materials needed

- Sign book

How to play

1. Choose a sign from the book that's easy to figure out.

2. Sign it for your nonsigning friends, and see if they can guess what it means.

3. Keep playing until your friends get hooked and want to learn sign language, too!

Bonus play

- Invite several friends to play and have a contest to see who can guess the most signs.

Teacher tip

- Demonstrate the signs for the class, and have them write down their answers. When they want to learn more signs, teach them more from the book!

Signless Charades

Can you play Charades without using signs? It's hard not to cheat!

NUMBER OF PLAYERS: 4 OR MORE

SIGN LEVEL: BEGINNER

MUST KNOW: GESTURES

Materials needed

- Paper and pencil
- Hat or box
- Three-minute timer

How to play

1. Divide into two teams.

2. Have players write down movie, song, or book titles on pieces of paper, then fold them, and put them in a hat or box.

3. Have one team player choose a paper from the other team's hat and act out the title for her own team, within the three-minute time frame.

4. Players can't use any sign language, only gestures. If a player accidentally uses a sign, the turn is over.

5. Keep track of how long it takes a team to guess an answer and write down the time.

6. Continue playing until all the papers are gone.

7. The team with the shortest total time wins the game.

Bonus play

- Play the game with no facial expressions.
- Play the game with no hands!

Teacher tip

- Divide the class into six-person teams, and use spelling words or phrases from your lessons to act out.

S-I-G-N-O

Play a game of sign language Bingo called S-I-G-N-O.

NUMBER OF PLAYERS: 2 OR MORE

SIGN LEVEL: INTERMEDIATE

MUST KNOW: FINGERSPELLING AND SOME SIGNS

Materials needed

- White poster board
- Black marker
- Photocopy of signs in the book
- Scissors
- Glue
- Bowl or hat
- Beans or other items to use as markers

How to play

1. Cut poster board into squares to make Bingo cards.
2. Draw a 5-by-5 grid on the squares.
3. Photocopy two sets of signs from the book.
4. Cut up the signs individually.

5. Glue one set of the signs on the cards, mixed up, so they're different on each card.

6. Mix up the other set and place them in a bowl or hat.

7. Pass out S-I-G-N-O cards and beans to each player.

8. Have someone pull a sign from the hat and sign it to the players.

9. If any player matches a sign on the card, he gets to put a bean on that spot.

10. Keep playing until one player fills in five spaces across, five spaces down, or five spaces diagonally. That player is the winner.

11. Exchange cards and play again.

Bonus play
- Have players fill in the entire card before they win.
- Fingerspell the words instead of signing them.

Teacher tip
- Change the cards each week, using new vocabulary words, to improve their skills.

Signs Around the World

Not all gestures and signs are the same around the world.

NUMBER OF PLAYERS: 2 OR MORE

SIGN LEVEL: BEGINNER

MUST KNOW: FINGERSPELLING

Materials needed

• Foreign signs from the book

How to play

See if you and your friends can guess what the following signs mean in other countries (see answers on page 194):

"Candy" in Italy means

    A. pretty girl

    B. sweet tooth

    C. happy person

Eyebrows raised in Peru means

    A. you look funny

    B. you owe me money

    C. you are crazy

Pulling your eyelid in Europe means

    A. be patient

    B. be quiet

    C. be alert

Tapping your nose in England means

    A. sticky

    B. secret

    C. silly

Flicking off your chin in Italy means

    A. buzz off

    B. watch out

    C. sit down

The sign for *crazy*—circling your finger at the side of your head—means crazy everywhere but the Netherlands, where it means

    A. airplane

    B. alarm

    C. telephone

The letter *F* means "fine" in the United States, but in France it means

    A. you're fun

    B. you're pretty

    C. you're a big zero

Nodding your head in the United States means "yes," while in Bulgaria it means

    A. I doubt it

    B. maybe

    C. no

Kissing your fingertips in Italy means

    A. terrible

    B. magnificent

    C. bizarre

A thumbs up in the United States means "good luck," but in Germany it means

    A. number 1

    B. hitchhike

    C. that-a-way

(If you want to say "good luck" in Germany, tuck your thumb in. And don't even think about signing a thumbs up in Nigeria. That's a big insult!)

Bonus play

- Make up some gestures and see whether your friends can guess what they mean.

Teacher tip

- Have the students find out what other gestures mean by going to the library and looking them up.
- Ask people from other countries to share some of their gestures, and let the kids guess what they mean.

Sign Search

This game is just like Hidden Word Search, only Sign Search uses the manual alphabet. Can you find the hidden words?

NUMBER OF PLAYERS: 1 OR MORE

SIGN LEVEL: BEGINNER

MUST KNOW: FINGERSPELLING

Materials needed
- Sign Search game provided

How to play
1. Find the familiar words listed below in this grid. Words may run up, down, horizontally, and backward—and they may overlap.

2. When you find a word, circle it, and cross off the corresponding word below.

Word List

ALPHABET	HEARING	PRACTICE
ASL	INTERPRET	READING
DEAF	LANGUAGE	SEE
EAR	LIPREAD	SHAPE
FACIAL	MANUAL	SIGN
FINGERSPELL	MIME	SOUND
GESTURE	NOD	SPEECH
HAND	POINT	

Sign Search

Bonus play

- When you're finished, make your own Sign Search for a friend.

Teacher tip

- Make copies of the Sign Search game for all the students, then have them work the puzzle.

Sign-Sync

Set your signs to music and watch your hands dance to the tunes.

NUMBER OF PLAYERS: 1 OR MORE

SIGN LEVEL: INTERMEDIATE TO ADVANCED

MUST KNOW: FINGERSPELLING AND SIGNS

Materials needed
- CDs or tapes
- Paper and pencil

How to play
1. Pick out your favorite slow songs from your CD collection.

2. Listen to the songs, and write down the words.

3. Practice the signs to the song until you know them well.

4. Turn on the music, and sign along to the song.

5. Practice several times; then videotape yourself signing to the music.

6. Watch the tape when you're finished—or give a live performance to your friends.

Bonus play
- Do a duet with a friend or have several backup signers.

Teacher tip
- Divide the class into groups of two to four and have them learn and perform a song in sign language. Videotape the performances, and play them back for the students.

Silence Is Golden

If you're a talker, this game will be a real challenge!

NUMBER OF PLAYERS: 2 OR MORE

SIGN LEVEL: BEGINNER

MUST KNOW: HOW TO KEEP QUIET!

Materials needed

- Timer

How to play

1. Spend a whole hour not talking, just signing.

2. If anyone accidentally says something, that player loses the game.

Bonus play

- The next time you play, don't sign, just mime!

Teacher tip

- Play the game in class and see whether the students can be quiet for a whole hour. That should be a challenge!

Silent Buzz

This game will help you with your math skills and your sign skills!

NUMBER OF PLAYERS: 2 OR MORE

SIGN LEVEL: BEGINNER

MUST KNOW: NUMBERS

Materials needed

- Paper and pencil

How to play

1. Players take turns counting in sign language, but each time a player comes to a number that is a 7 or multiple of 7, she must fingerspell the word *buzz*.

2. If a player forgets to sign *buzz* when a 7 or multiple of 7 appears, she loses a point.

3. Continue until all players reach 100.

4. Count up points to see who wins the game.

Bonus play

- Play again, using 3 and multiples of 3 for the "buzz" word.

Teacher tip

- Adjust the game to practice multiplication tables or other math skills.

Did You Know?

Most deaf children in public schools are "mainstreamed," which means they spend some or all of the day in hearing classrooms. Can you think of how many ways this benefits a deaf child? What about a hearing child?

Silly Story Signs

Can you catch the mistakes when a story is signed?

NUMBER OF PLAYERS: 2 OR MORE

SIGN LEVEL: INTERMEDIATE TO ADVANCED

MUST KNOW: FINGERSPELLING AND SIGNS

Materials needed
- Storybooks

How to play
1. Get a popular child's picture book from the bookshelf or library.

2. One player must sign and fingerspell the story to the other players, but he must make a mistake as he signs. For example, if he chooses "The Three Little Pigs," he might sign and fingerspell, "Once upon a time there were three little hogs."

3. The other player must try to guess when a mistake is made and correct it.

4. Take turns signing picture books and making mistakes to be corrected. This should offer a few laughs as you play.

Bonus play
- Play the game using song lyrics.

Teacher tip
- Play the game to help the kids prepare for a test, by signing and fingerspelling text information, and making mistakes the kids must correct.

Snap, Clap, and Sign

Try to come up with a sign when it's your turn to snap and clap.

NUMBER OF PLAYERS: 2 OR MORE

SIGN LEVEL: INTERMEDIATE

MUST KNOW: FINGERSPELLING AND SOME SIGNS

Materials needed

- Paper and pencil

How to play

1. Players sit on the floor, opposite one another.

2. One player chooses a category, such as "snacks," "clothing," "drinks," "TV shows," "cars," and so on.

3. On the word "Go!" the player snaps her fingers and claps her hands in unison and then signs a word from the category on the third beat.

4. The next player must keep the beat, snapping, clapping, and signing a new word from the category.

5. Play continues as players take turns using new words from the category each time.

6. If a player cannot come up with a new word, she gets a point.

7. Choose another category and play again.

8. The player with the most points loses the game.

Bonus play

- Pick up the beat and make the game go faster, to increase the tension.

Teacher tip

- Divide the class into small groups of four or five, and have the students use topics from the lessons as categories.

Telephone Tag

You'll need a few friends to play this game of mixed-up messages.

NUMBER OF PLAYERS: 3 OR MORE

SIGN LEVEL: INTERMEDIATE

MUST KNOW: FINGERSPELLING AND SOME SIGNS

Materials needed

- Paper and pencil

How to play

1. One player thinks of a phrase to sign and fingerspell to the player next to her, while the rest of the players are not looking.

2. The second player passes the message on to the next player, using fingerspelling and signs, making sure the remaining players are not looking.

3. Play continues until the last player receives the message. He must repeat the message to the group and see whether it's the same as the original message. It's usually all mixed up!

Bonus play

- Fingerspell words instead of sentences; see if the messages remain the same.

Teacher tip

- Break the class into groups of six to eight, and have them practice sentences from their texts.

Twenty Signs

Guess the person, place, or thing using sign language and fingerspelling.

NUMBER OF PLAYERS: 2 OR MORE

SIGN LEVEL: INTERMEDIATE TO ADVANCED

MUST KNOW: FINGERSPELLING AND SIGNS

Materials needed

- Paper and pencil

How to play

1. One player thinks of a person, place, or thing and signs to the other players what category it is.

2. The next player gets to ask a question in sign language. For example, if the category is "person," the question might be, "Is this person alive?"

3. After the question is answered, the player may guess the answer.

4. If he's incorrect, play continues until one of the players guesses the correct answer, or twenty questions have been asked.

5. Take turns thinking of a person, place, or thing, and guessing in sign language.

6. Keep score to see who gets the correct answer in the fewest questions.

Bonus play

- Give the player a hint each time he asks a question.
- Restrict the game to famous people, real or fictional.
- Make the game more challenging by having the players guess the correct answer in ten questions.

Teacher tip

- Break the class into small groups of four to five, and have them use people, places, or things from their lessons.

Answers

Page 148 (Decode the Code)

1. Sign language is fun to learn.

2. I want to be an interpreter someday.

3. My best friend is deaf.

4. Do you know how to fingerspell?

5. Deaf people can do anything.

6. My sign language is getting better.

7. Can you spell your name?

8. I can see the doorbell ring.

9. Can you talk without using your voice?

10. My deaf friends call me on a TTY.

Page 157 (Guess the Gesture)

- Victory or peace
- Power
- Okay
- Live long and prosper
- Good job
- Hang loose
- Hook 'em horns
- Time out
- I love you

Page 181 (Signs Around the World)

- A: pretty girl
- B: you owe me money
- C: be alert
- B: be quiet
- A: buzz off
- C: telephone
- C: you're a big zero
- C: no
- B: magnificent
- A: number one

Page 184 (Sign Search)

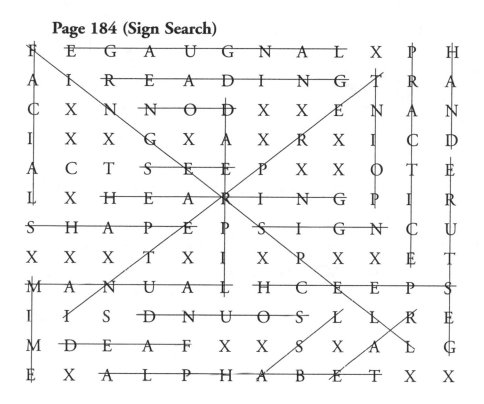

Glossary

Some of the terms used in the book may be new to you, so we've defined them for you here.

Ambidextrous: The ability to use both hands equally, without a dominant hand.

American Sign Language (ASL): The native language used by the Deaf community in the United States, with its own distinct grammatical structure. It is visual rather than auditory and is composed of specific hand shapes and movements.

Amplification: The use of hearing aids to provide as much sound as possible for a deaf person who has some hearing.

Body language: Using your arms, legs, head, and body to communicate along with your signs.

Captioning: Provides deaf people with translations for dialogue and important noises on TV. The captions appear on the screen using a device called a *decoder*.

Cochlear implant: A device implanted near the ear to increase the ability to hear for some deaf people.

Deaf community: A group of people who share similar language, culture, beliefs, and attitudes. Both deaf people and hearing people may belong to the Deaf community.

Dominant hand: The hand signers use for signing. If you are right-handed, that is your dominant hand. If you are left-handed, that is your dominant hand.

Facial expression: Using your face to express your feelings as you speak and sign, by lifting your eyebrows, frowning, smiling, grimacing, nodding, shaking your head, and so on.

Fingerspelling: Forming words by spelling the letters of the manual alphabet.

Gesture: Acting out or miming a concept to communicate with another person.

Hearing impairment: A degree of hearing loss, from mild to hard of hearing to profoundly deaf.

Interpreter: A hearing person trained in sign language who translates spoken language into sign for deaf people, and sign language into speech for hearing people.

Lipreading/speechreading: The ability to understand speech by watching the shape of the lips, mouth, teeth, and tongue.

Manual alphabet: Each letter of the alphabet as represented by a different hand shape.

Oral deaf: A person who uses speech and lipreading, not sign language, to communicate.

SEE signs: Stands for "signing exact English"; uses signs to represent English grammar, syntax, and vocabulary.

Signal dog/hearing ear dog: A dog trained in sign language to alert a deaf person to important sounds in the environment.

Signed English: Using vocabulary from ASL in English format, primarily for hearing people learning sign language when communicating with deaf people.

TDD/TTY: Teletypewriter device for the deaf; a device that enables deaf people to use the telephone. When the phone rings, the receiver is placed on a coupler attached to the TTY. The deaf person uses a keyboard to communicate and receives message on a small screen.

Total communication: The use of sign language, speech, lipreading, gestures, paper and pencil, and anything else that helps with communication.

Resources

To find out more about sign language, deafness, and other related topics, look for the following at your local library, bookstore, college bookstore, Internet bookstore, or Internet search engine.

A Basic Course in American Sign Language by Tom Humphries, Carol Padden, and Terrence J. O'Rourke (TJ Publishers, 1989). An introductory sign language book used by most schools teaching sign language.

American Sign Language (ASL) Dictionary Online, dww.deafworldweb.org/asl. A dictionary for American Sign Language.

Animated American Sign Language Dictionary, www.bconnex.net/~randys. An animated visual representation of ASL.

ASL Fingerspelling Dictionary, where.com/scott.net/asl. Practice fingerspelling the manual alphabet on-line.

Deaf Culture Our Way by Roy Holcomb, Samuel Holcomb, and Thomas Holcomb (Dawn Sign Press, 1994). Anecdotes from the Deaf community.

Deafinitions for Signlets by Ken Glickman (DiKen Products, 1986). A book of colorful ways to use newly created signs.

Fairy Tales I, videotape by Paul Chamberlain. Fairy tales told in American Sign Language, using deaf storytellers, with voice-over. Available through Amazon.com.

Gestures: The Do's and Taboos of Body Language around the World by Roger E. Axtell (Wiley, 1998). How body language and gestures differ around the world.

Harris Communications, www.harriscommunications.com. A catalog of books, games, jewelry, toys, and other sign language–related materials.

Joy of Signing Puzzle Book by Linda Lascelle Hillebrand (Gospel Publishing House, 1989). A book of puzzles and games to play with fingerspelling and sign.

Land before Time, videotape by Don Bluth. The classic story told in sign language. Available through Amazon.com.

Signing Exact English by Gerilee Gustason and Esther Zawolkow (Modern Signs Press, 1993). A dictionary of SEE signs that incorporate English and sign language.

Silence Is Golden—Sometimes by Roy Holcomb (Dawn Sign Press, 1985). Some of the hazards of being deaf, told with humor.

Songs in Sign by S. Harold Collins, Kathy Kifer, and Dahna Solar (Garlic Press, 1995). Learn your favorite songs in sign language.

Index

Hearing impairment, 197
Hearing people, signing by, comparison with deaf people, 138
Heart, sign for, 113
Home
    signs for parts of, 59–64
    word sign for, 60
Homework, sign, 119
Horse, sign for, 40–41
Horseback riding, sign for, 78
Hot, sign for, 133
Hot dog, sign for, 52
House, sign for, 60
100, number sign for, 27
Hurry, sign for, 107

I

I, how to fingerspell the letter, 8
Ice cream, sign for, 53
Interpreter, 197
    career opportunities, 3
    definition, 2–3

J

J, how to fingerspell the letter, 8
Jacket, sign for, 66
Juice, sign for, 55
Jump, sign for, 103

K

K, how to fingerspell the letter, 8
Keller, Helen, 144
Kid, sign for, 37
Kiss, sign for, 96
Kitchen, sign for, 61

L

L, how to fingerspell the letter, 9
Last week, sign for, 130
Laugh, sign for, 136
"Laughing Fingers" game, 159–160
Learn, sign for, 116
"Letter Out" game, 160–161
Library, sign for, 117
Lie, sign for, 135
Like, sign for, 98
Lion, sign for, 42

"Lip Service" game, 162
Lipreading, 24, 70, 122, 140, 197
    game for, 162
Look, sign for, 106
Love, sign for, 94
Lunch, sign for, 49

M

M, how to fingerspell the letter, 9
Mad, sign for, 95
Mainstreaming, of deaf children in classrooms, 188
Man, sign for, 36
Manual Alphabet, 197
Manual alphabet. *See also*
    Fingerspelling
    one-handed and two-handed, comparison, 9
    overview, 3–14
"Match-a-Sign" game, 163–164
Me, word sign for, 33
Meat, sign for, 51
Milk, sign for, 55
"Mime in Time" game, 164–165
Mirror, sign for, 63
"Missing Fingers" game, 165–166
Mom, sign for, 33
Monday, sign for, 126
Money amounts, how to sign, 29
Monkey, sign for, 40, 43
Monster, sign for, 134
Morning, sign for, 125
Mouse, sign for, 45
Mouth, sign for, 111
Movie, sign for, 82
"Movie Signs" game, 167
Multiples, how to sign, 99
Music
    use in game, 186
    sign for, 83

N

N, how to fingerspell the letter, 9
Name sign, 58
"Name That Tune" game, 168–169
Next week, sign for, 130
Night, sign for, 126
9, number sign for, 20
19, number sign for, 24

90, number sign for, 27
No, sign for, 91
Noon, sign for, 125
Nose, sign for, 111
Number signs, 15–30
"Number Signs" game, 169–170

O

O, how to fingerspell the letter, 10
Occupations, how to make signs for, 114
OK, sign for, 90
1, number sign for, 18
Open hand, as basic hand shape, 16
"Oppo-Sign" game, 170–171
Oral deaf, 197
Oral schools, 115
Orange, color sign for, 71

P

P, how to fingerspell the letter, 10
Pajamas, sign for, 68
Pants, sign for, 65–66
Paper, sign for, 119
Parents
    teaching sign language to children, 31
    sign for, 38
Party, sign for, 84
Past, signs to designate the, 130
Payphones, and TTYs, 193
People, signs for, 31–39
Person, sign for, 110
Person signs, 114
Photography, sign for, 81
Pig, sign for, 45
Pink, sign for color, 73
Pizza, sign for, 51
Play, sign for, 85
Please, sign for, 89
Plurals, how to sign, 99
Pointing, role of, 74
Present, signs to designate the, 130
Purple, sign for, 72

Q

Q, how to fingerspell the letter, 10
Question, signing to form a, 39

About the Author

Penny Warner has written more than thirty books, including five books in the Connor Westphal mystery series, featuring a deaf amateur sleuth. Her first book, *Dead Body Language,* was nominated for an Agatha Award and won a Macavity Award for Best First Mystery. She writes a series for middle-grade readers featuring thirteen-year-old scouts who solve mysteries.

Warner has a bachelor's degree in child development and a master's degree in special education and teaches child development at Dialdo Valley College in San Ramon, California.

She has also taught sign language and special education classes, preschool classes for deaf children, and creative writing. She has appeared on television talk shows and wrote a weekly newspaper column. Warner lives in Danville, California, with her husband and two children.